Apple

Cucumber

Wheat

Pumpkin

Cherries

Peas

Cotton

CONTENTS

Seed Magic 6

What Is Inside a Seed? 10

How Seeds Are Made 14

Seeds on the Move 19

Fruits of Many Kinds 26

Useful Seeds 30

A Garden of Your Own 36

Surprising Seeds 42

Index 44

Library of Congress Cataloging in Publication Data

Shuttlesworth, Dorothy Edwards.
  The hidden magic of seeds.

  Includes index.
  SUMMARY: Describes different kinds and uses of
seeds, what they are, and how they grow and move.
Makes suggestions for planting seeds in home gardens.
  1. Seeds–Juvenile literature. [1. Seeds] I. Title.
QK661.S48   582'.03'34   76-3328
ISBN 0-87857-128-0

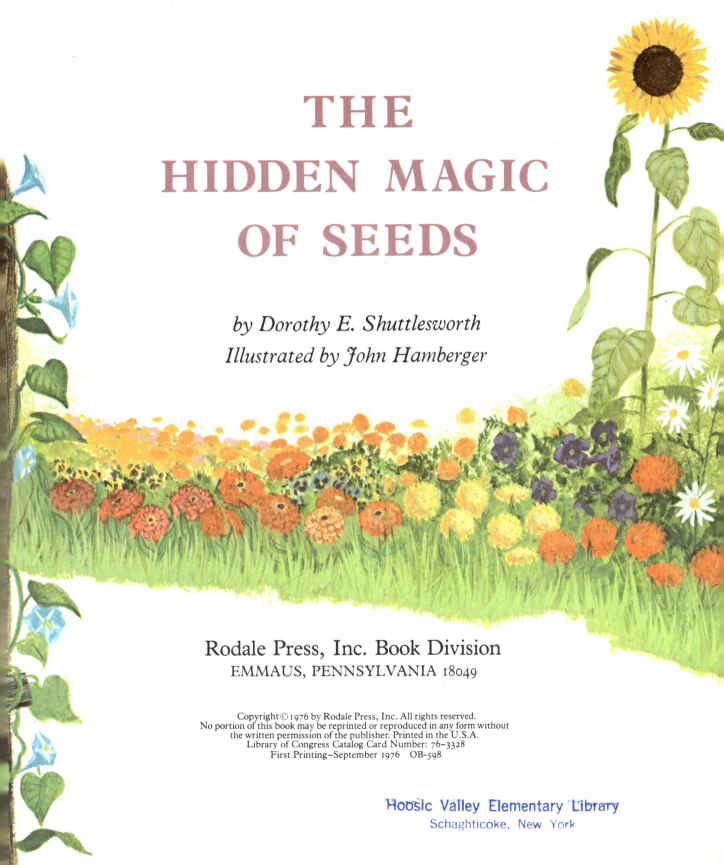

THE HIDDEN MAGIC OF SEEDS

by Dorothy E. Shuttlesworth
Illustrated by John Hamberger

Rodale Press, Inc. Book Division
EMMAUS, PENNSYLVANIA 18049

The winged seed of a maple tree starts
growing into a beautiful new tree.

Seed Magic

Have you ever watched a magician pull a rabbit
out of a hat?

We all know that magicians use make-believe
when they entertain people in this way. They cannot
pull a rabbit out of an empty hat without the help
of tricks which the audience cannot see. But when
we put a tiny, dry seed into soil, and it develops into
a beautiful plant, this is true magic. No tricks are
needed to make it happen.

You can set up a "magic show" of your own by planting a seed where you can watch it develop.

A grapefruit seed is a good one to choose. Take a seed from a freshly opened grapefruit and allow it to dry for a couple of days. Then soak it in water overnight. The next morning it will be ready for planting. Use a clear drinking glass for this so you can see what happens.

Fill the glass almost to the top with potting soil that is damp but not wet. Now put in the grapefruit seed—an inch or two down in the soil is deep enough. But place it very close to the side of the glass so you can watch it grow.

You may wonder as you plant seeds how they should be placed in the soil. Is there an "up" side and a "down" side to each seed? Might seeds be planted "upside down"? Will roots and stems have a hard time growing in the right direction?

There is no danger of this happening. Not only grapefruit seeds, but all seeds have the power to grow in just the right way. No matter how they are placed in the soil, the roots grow down. The stem grows up.

Wild hazelnut seed

A few days after you plant the grapefruit seed, the "show" starts. The seed has begun to sprout! You can see tiny roots growing down into the soil and a stem growing up.

Just keep the soil damp, and leave the glass in a bright, but not sunny, spot. In a few more days the stem will reach the top of the soil and break through. The roots will fan out and grow deeper into the soil.

After the first leaves appear, you can move the little plant, with the soil around it, into a flowerpot. It will continue to grow if you keep it in a warm place where sunlight can reach it several hours a day, and if you make sure the soil is always moist. In a few months the plant will look like a pretty little tree with shiny green leaves and a woody stem.

What is Inside a Seed?

How do such hard little objects as seeds, which seem to have no more life than a stone, work their magic? Where do the roots and stems come from?

Under the hard outside coating of every seed is a tiny baby plant. This "baby" is made up of cells. Some cells will grow into leaves and stems, and other cells will grow into roots. Tiny amounts of food are also stored in the seed.

Seeds can remain hard and dry for weeks, months, or even years, without becoming active in any way. We might like to think about them as waiting to be touched by a magic wand to bring them to life.

This "wand" is water.

The food that is stored in a seed cannot be used until it has been dissolved by water. Then the baby plant is fed and begins to swell.

Meanwhile, the water also has softened the seed's hard coating, and the little plant growing inside can burst through it.

When all the stored food has been used, the newly sprouted roots, stem, and leaves will help feed the plant so that it can continue to grow.

Wild hazelnut

Too much water.

Seeds are planted too deep.

After water has made a seed come alive, the seed must have air. It needs oxygen from the air to live.

For this reason, seeds must not be planted too far down in the soil. If air cannot reach the seeds, they will be smothered and die.

And although they need water, if seeds are covered with too much water, they will drown.

If you want to have a good look at the inside of a seed, find a dry lima bean in your kitchen cupboard. Soak it in water overnight. Then carefully split it open. Inside you can see a tiny stem, leaves, and stored food.

Lima beans are large seeds, so the parts can be seen clearly.

A lima bean seed can be made to sprout without being planted in soil. Line a glass jar with a piece of dripping wet blotting paper, and push several beans gently between the blotting paper and glass. Within a week you should see the roots and stem of new plants sprout and grow.

First the roots will start sprouting, then the stems. Remember to keep the blotting paper moist.

How Seeds Are Made

Many flowers are so pretty we may think that their whole purpose is to bring beauty to our world. But a flower also has a very different purpose. It is the "workshop" of a plant, the place where seeds are produced.

In some kinds of flowers you can easily see parts that work together to make seeds. In other kinds, those parts do not show plainly, but you may be able to see them through a magnifying glass.

14

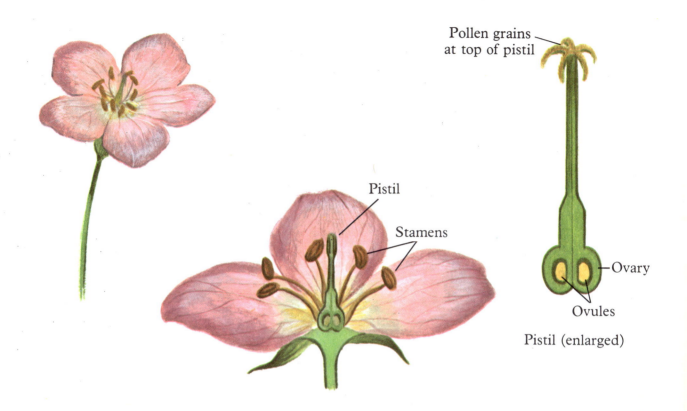

Pollen grains at top of pistil

Pistil

Stamens

Ovary

Ovules

Pistil (enlarged)

One very important part of a flower is the pistil. There may be a single pistil in a flower, or more than one, depending on the kind of plant.

At the bottom of each pistil is an ovary in which tiny beginning-seeds, called ovules, are formed.

Each ovule contains an egg cell. But before the egg cells are able to grow, something almost magical must happen to them. They must be touched by tubes that grow from pollen grains.

The yellow pollen grains, which play such an important part in the making of seeds, grow at the top of little stalks in the flower called stamens.

Stamens are often in the same flower as the pistil, forming a ring around it. But on some kinds of plants, the pistils and stamens grow in separate flowers.

The pistil flowers and the stamen flowers may both be on one plant. Or one kind of flower may grow on one plant and the other on a separate plant.

Stamen
flower

Corn has stamen flowers
and pistil flowers on one plant.

Pistil
flower

Pollen grains must get from the stamens to the pistils in some way. If the stamen flowers and pistil flowers are on the same plant, the pollen may simply fall from one flower to the other. Sometimes the pollen is carried to the pistils by wind. Sometimes it is carried on the legs or backs of insects that visit the flowers.

Once a pollen grain has settled on the top of a pistil, it starts to grow out in the form of a hairlike tube. In this shape it works its way down through the pistil until it reaches the ovary at the bottom. In the ovary, a small living part of the pollen tube actually goes into the ovule.

In a peach blossom, pistil and stamens are in one flower.

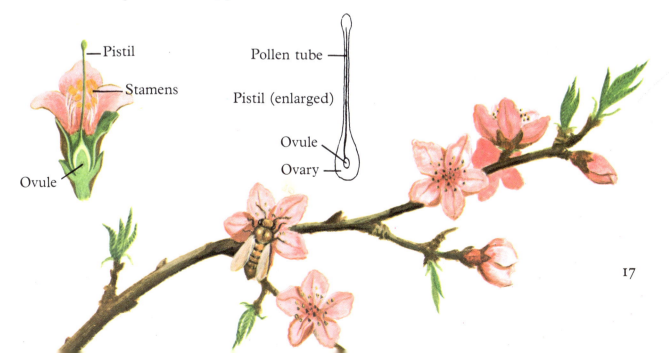

Pistil

Stamens

Ovule

Pollen tube

Pistil (enlarged)

Ovule

Ovary

17

Ovules

Ovary

Garden Pea

Apple

Cherry

Tomato

Seeds are beginning to form
in each of these flowers.

When pollen and ovule have joined, the ovule begins to grow. It then develops into a seed within the ovary. Seeds remain inside the ovary and are protected by it until the ovary ripens.

The purpose of the flower has now been carried out. It has provided seeds that can grow into new plants that will be just like the plants that made them.

But seeds must get into soil in order to develop. Sometimes they simply drop near the plant on which they grew, and new plants may start growing from them. Some plants scatter their seeds, however, so they are able to grow at a distance from the flowers that produced them.

Seeds on the Move

Some of nature's ways of planting are very simple. To see one of the scattering methods, look at a pansy.

After the flower has finished its work making seeds, the ovary pops open and the seeds are shot out to the ground.

Some other seeds are shot out with much greater force. Witch-hazel seeds go many feet from the plant that made them.

When the ripened ovary of a sandbox tree bursts, the noise is like that of a pistol shot, and the seeds are scattered far and wide.

Pansy

Witch-hazel

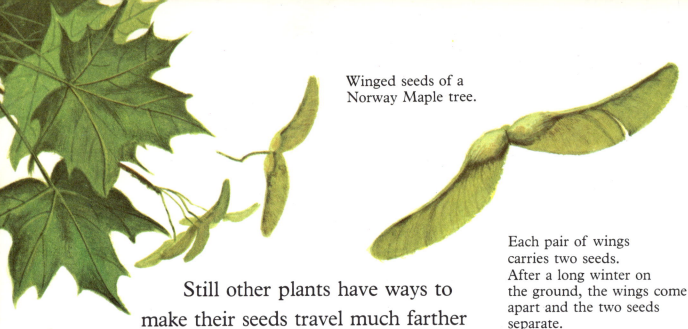

Winged seeds of a
Norway Maple tree.

Each pair of wings
carries two seeds.
After a long winter on
the ground, the wings come
apart and the two seeds
separate.

Still other plants have ways to make their seeds travel much farther than those that are shot. Some develop wings. Some grow feathery tufts. Some grow spines or hooks.

To see wings in action, let's look at the seeds of a maple tree.

On maple trees, two seeds grow side by side, and each has a thin, paperlike wing extending from it. This combination makes a perfect little flying machine that can be carried along by a strong wind or even a light breeze. It twirls around and around, gradually moving toward the earth, where it finally settles.

20

Milkweed seeds.

Milkweed seed pod.

Dandelion seeds.

Dandelion and milkweed seeds have silky tufts attached to them. These, too, are caught by passing breezes, and sail long distances in the air.

Cotton seeds have a covering of white fibers. When the fruit ripens and opens, the fibers hang out. Wind can carry the fibers away with their seeds.

Seeds with hooks or spines attached to the outside covering need animals or people to help them move. The hooks and spines catch on to fur, hair, clothing, or almost anything that touches them. Later they are brushed off. If this happens at a good growing spot, the seeds will produce new plants.

Other seeds receive different kinds of help from animals.

Squirrels, although they do not know it, often are working for trees when they bury nuts. The squirrels intend to store the nuts, to use them as food at some later time. But buried nuts cannot always be found. So, instead of being dug up and eaten, they may sprout and grow.

A small acorn buried in this way can produce a wonderful oak tree with a huge trunk and many wide-spreading branches on which new acorns will grow.

As years go by, the difference in size between the great tree and the little acorn that was planted by a squirrel is amazing. It is almost like magic!

Other furry animals, and birds too, spread seeds because they eat berries and fruits that have seeds in them. The seeds pass through the body of the animal without being harmed, and after a while they drop to the ground.

Many seeds use water for travel. The seeds may fall into a stream or a lake or an ocean. Or they may be carried along by heavy rains and flood waters. Some seeds can stay in water for quite a long time before they reach soil and start growing.

Acorn

Black walnut

Pumpkin

Pear

Apple

Cucumber

Tomato

Fruits of Many Kinds

A fruit is the ripened ovary of any kind of flower. It may be hard and dry, like an acorn or a walnut, or it may be soft and juicy.

Some of the soft fruits, such as apples and pears, are always called fruits. Many others, such as cucumbers, pumpkins, and tomatoes, are usually called vegetables. But they are really fruits, too.

These fruits, and others that have more than one seed, develop from flowers that have more than one ovule.

Some kinds of seeds have special aids for water travel. The seed of a coconut tree, inside its protective fruit, may fall into the ocean and drift along for many miles before reaching land. But the seed is not damaged by this, for the outer covering of the fruit is very thick and completely waterproof. Inside the covering are many lightweight fibers which help the fruit to float.

Hard outer covering of coconut fruit

Seed

Seed coat

Fibers

Sometimes the fruit of a coconut palm is washed up on a beach. After a while the hard outer covering cracks open and the seed inside may sprout and grow into a new tree.

Cherries

Cherry pit

Peach

Outside layer

Inside layer (pit)

Plums

Peach pit

Hard covering

Seed

Plum pit (Seed is inside)

The fruits of such grasses as rice and wheat, called grain, are one-seed fruits.

One-seed fruits develop from a flower that has only one ovule.

With some one-seed fruits, such as cherries, peaches, and plums, the ovary that surrounds the ovule develops into two layers. The outside layer becomes the fleshy part of the fruit and the skin that covers it. The inside layer forms a hard covering around the seed. You know this part as the pit.

Raspberry
blossom

Pistils

Fruitlets

When a flower has many pistils, it can develop many little fruitlets. This is because the ovary of each pistil produces its own tiny fruit. Fruits such as raspberries and blackberries come from flowers with many pistils.

Raspberries

Blackberries

The pod of a pea plant is its fruit. The seeds hang inside, along one edge of the pod.

Pea pod

Seeds

There are many different kinds of fruits. Some are large, some are small. They are different in color and in shape. Some are rough outside, some are smooth. Some are hard, some are soft. Some have one seed, some have many.

But all fruits have only one purpose for the plants on which they grow. That purpose is to protect the seeds inside until they are ready to go back into the soil and start new plants.

Orange

Green pepper

Apricot

Cantaloupe

Walnut

Almond

Hazelnut

Peanut

29

Acorns

White Oak

Useful Seeds

Thousands of years ago, when people lived in caves, they probably did not think about the "magic" of seeds. Yet these people knew how to make use of seeds. They ate the seeds of many plants they found growing wild. And they ate the stems, roots, and leaves that the seeds produced.

Gradually people started to take seeds from plants they liked very much and put them in the ground near the place where they lived. When the next growing season came around, they did not have to search for their favorite plants again. That is really how gardening began.

Marsh Marigold

American Lotus

Seed pod

Cattail

American Indians, long ago, ate some seeds and
planted others. They picked acorns from the ground
and from the branches of oak trees. They removed
the hard coverings and turned these seeds into useful
meal.

They used the oil pressed from the seeds of
water lilies to mix with their food. Or they roasted
the seeds and then ground them into mush which
was good to eat.

The seeds of many kinds of grasses were also used in those long-ago days. Indians ground some of them into meal that they could either eat raw or turn into a paste for cooking.

The most amazing of all grass seeds that Indians used were the seeds of corn. The Indians learned to plant the seeds that we call kernels. These produced plants that were even better than the plants that grew wild.

Corn seed sprouting

Today we use the seeds of wheat as well as corn for food. Flour and many cereals are made from wheat grains. The covering of the seed is called bran.

We eat corn seeds cooked or popped. And we use the oil squeezed from corn seeds in many ways.

The seeds of the rice plant feed billions of people every year. There are important minerals in the brown seed covering. But in some parts of the world these seed coverings are removed before rice is sold at the market because many people like their rice to be white.

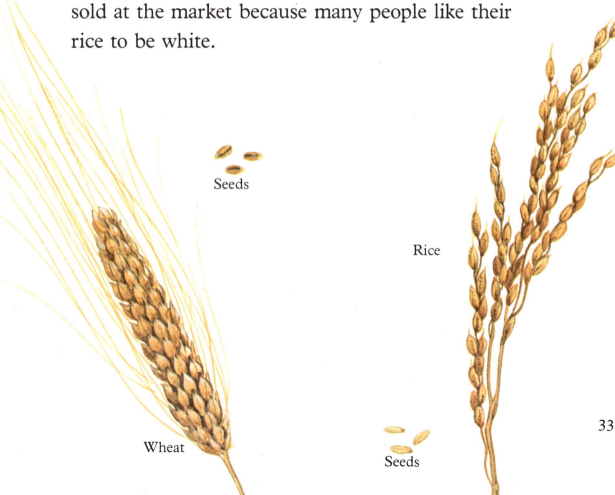

Seeds

Rice

Wheat

Seeds

33

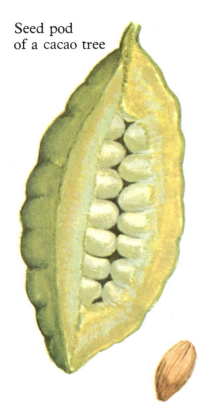

Seed pod
of a cacao tree

Seeds are used to flavor some
of the tastiest things we eat and drink.

The seeds of the cacao tree are
turned into chocolate for flavoring
cocoa, candy, and many kinds of food.

The seeds of kola trees are used
in making cola drinks.

Coffee beans are the seeds of
coffee plants. After the beans are
roasted, they are used to make coffee.

Ripe cocoa seed

Seed of kola tree

Coffee berries

Seed (coffee bean)

Cross section
of coffee berry

Cotton seed

Cotton plant

Cotton seeds are useful in two ways. The white hairs that cover them are made into yarn and cloth. And the seeds themselves contain oil which is used for cooking.

Seeds are used in so many ways it might seem that plants produced them just for people to use. But the plant's real purpose in making seeds is to reproduce itself.

A Garden of Your Own

The best way to be really close to seed magic is to plant a garden, raising vegetables to eat and flowers for their beauty.

You can do this indoors, or you can start seeds indoors and later move plants outside. Or all the gardening may be done indoors or outdoors.

You can buy packages of seeds that will give you the plants you want. On each package you will find instructions that tell you when and how to plant the seeds.

Plant seeds.

Cover lightly with soil.

Watch for sprouts.

Make room for plants to grow.

Radish seeds are interesting to plant because they develop fast. The part of the plant that we eat is the root.

Indoors you may plant the seeds in potting soil in a flat wooden box or a flowerpot seven inches or more across. Radish seeds need only a light covering of the soil. Keep them close to a sunny window and give them plenty of water.

In a few days, tiny plants should push up through the soil. If they are too close together, pull some up so there is at least an inch of space around each plant.

Radish

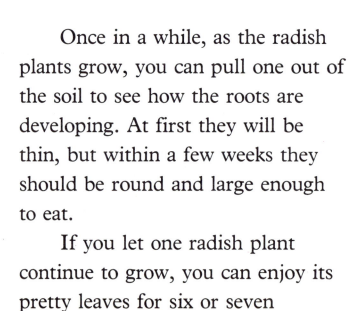

Once in a while, as the radish plants grow, you can pull one out of the soil to see how the roots are developing. At first they will be thin, but within a few weeks they should be round and large enough to eat.

If you let one radish plant continue to grow, you can enjoy its pretty leaves for six or seven months. Then small white or purple flowers will appear, ready to create a new crop of seeds.

38

Tomato seeds are another good choice for home gardeners. If you want plants ready for an outdoor garden, the seeds should be planted indoors late in the winter.
About a week later, small plants will begin to show above the soil. In about four more weeks, these may be moved to a sunny spot outdoors, if the soil is warm enough.

Dried tomato seed ready for planting.

Tomato flower

Small green fruit

Fruit grows larger.

When the tomato plants have been growing outdoors for four or five days, you will begin to see small yellow flowers appear among the leaves.

A few days later there will be another change as the flowers start turning into small green fruits.

When these grow and become red, you know they are ready to be picked. As you slice a tomato, you will see many seeds.

If one of these tomatoes became too ripe and fell to the ground before you had a chance to pick it, the seeds would plant themselves. In the spring you would find new little tomato plants starting to grow where the seeds fell.

A number of different kinds of seeds will give you pretty flowers: nasturtiums, petunias, and marigolds, to name only a few.

You can buy seeds for these and many other lovely flowers at the supermarket or at a garden center. Some five-and-dime variety stores sell them too.

All these plants need lots of sunshine, either at a window or outdoors. And the soil around them must be kept moist if you want your flowers to grow and be beautiful.

Nasturtium

Petunias

Marigolds

Nasturtium seed   Petunia seeds   Marigold seeds

Surprising Seeds

Seeds are full of surprises. It is true that every seed holds the beginning of a new plant. But you cannot tell by looking at a seed just what to expect.

A milkweed seed is larger than the seed of a giant sequoia tree. Yet the milkweed plant grows only a few feet tall. Sequoias reach heights of three hundred feet or more. They would tower over an apartment building thirty-five stories high.

Milkweed seed

Sequoia seeds

There are thousands of different kinds of seeds,
and they grow in many climates all over the world.
They grow into many different kinds of plants.

But all of them are alike in one way.

Each seed can grow into a plant that will
produce new seeds. And all these new seeds can produce
plants like the plant that made them.

Each seed, large or small, wherever it grows, has
its own magic hidden inside.

43

Index

Acorns, 22-23, 31
Animals, seeds spread by, 21-24

Birds, seeds spread by, 24
Blackberries, 28
Bran, 33

Cacao tree, 34
Cells within seeds, 10
Cereals, 33
Cherries, 27
Chocolate, 34
Coconut-tree seeds, 25
Coffee beans, 34
Cola drinks, 34
Corn seeds, 32
Cotton seeds, 21, 35

Dandelion seeds, 21

Egg cells, 15, 17-18

Feathery tufts, seeds with, 20
Flour, 33
Flowerpot, planting in a, 9
Flowers: garden, 41; as
   producers of seeds, 14-18,
   26-28; radish, 38; tomato, 40
Food: made from seeds, 31-35;
   stored in seeds, 10-11
Fruits, 26-29

Gardening, 30, 36-41
Grain, 27, 33
Grapefruit seed, 7-9

Grasses, 27, 32

Hooks, seeds with, 20, 21

Indians, American, 31-32
Insect-carried pollen, 17

Kernels. *See* Corn seeds
Kola tree, 34

Lima bean seed, 13

Maple tree, 20
Meal from seeds, 31, 32
Milkweed seeds, 21, 42

Oak tree, 22-23, 31
Oil from seeds, 31
One-seed fruits, 27
Ovary, 15, 17-18, 19, 26-28
Overwatering, 12
Ovule, 15, 17, 18, 26-27
Oxygen, 12

Packaged seeds, 36, 41
Pansy, 14, 19
Peaches, 27
Pea plant, 28
Pistil, 15-17, 28
Pit, 27
Placing seeds in soil, 8,
   37, 39
Planting a seed, 7-9
Plums, 27
Pod, pea, 28

Pollen grains, 15-17
Potting soil, 7, 37

Radishes, how to grow, 37-38
Raspberries, 28
Rice, 27, 33
Roasted seeds, 31
Roots, how they grow, 8

Sandbox tree, 19
Scattering seeds, 18-25
Seeds, how they are made, 14
Sequoia tree, 42
Silky tufts, seeds with, 21
Softening seeds, 11
Soil: moistness of, 7, 9, 41;
   placing seeds in, 8, 37, 39
Spines, seeds with, 20, 21
Sprouting, 9, 13
Squirrels, 22
Stamens, 15, 16-17
Stems, how they grow, 8

Tomatoes, how to grow, 39-40

Useful seeds, 30-35

Water, 10-12; seeds carried by,
   24-25; soaking seeds in, 7
Wheat, 27, 33
Wild plants, 30, 32
Wind-carried pollen, 17
Wind, seeds spread by, 21
Wings, seeds with, 20
Witch-hazel seeds, 19

Lima Beans

Grapefruit

Pear

Blackberries

Tomato

Petunia

Raspberries

Radish

Corn